THAT ROCKS!

METAMORPHIC ROCKS

By Maria Nelson

Gareth Stevens
Publishing

Please visit our website, www.garethstevens.com. For a free color catalog of all our high-quality books, call toll free 1-800-542-2595 or fax 1-877-542-2596.

Library of Congress Cataloging-in-Publication Data

Library of Congress Cataloging-in-Publication Data

Nelson, Maria.
Metamorphic rocks / Maria Nelson.
    p. cm. — (That rocks!)
Includes index.
ISBN 978-1-4339-8318-4 (pbk.)
ISBN 978-1-4339-8319-1 (6-pack)
ISBN 978-1-4339-8317-7 (library binding)
1. Metamorphic rocks—Juvenile literature. I. Title.
QE475.A2N47 2014
552'.4—dc23

                                2012047153

First Edition

Published in 2014 by
Gareth Stevens Publishing
111 East 14th Street, Suite 349
New York, NY 10003

Copyright © 2014 Gareth Stevens Publishing

Designer: Katelyn Londino
Editor: Kristen Rajczak

Photo credits: Cover, p. 1 David Woods/Shutterstock.com; p. 5 Doug Lemke/Shutterstock.com; p. 7 James Balog/ Stone/Getty Images; p. 9 © iStockphoto.com/seraficus; p. 11 Luis Castaneda Inc./The Image Bank/Getty Images; p. 13 MarkVanDykePhotography/Shutterstock.com; p. 15 MIXA/Getty Images; p. 17 LesPalenik/Shutterstock.com; p. 19 Mirka Moksha/Shutterstock.com; p. 20 (inset) Marafona/Shutterstock.com.

Printed in the United States of America

CPSIA compliance information: Batch #CS13GS: For further information contact Gareth Stevens, New York, New York at 1-800-542-2595.

CONTENTS

Words in the glossary appear in **bold** type the first time they are used in the text.

ALWAYS ADAPTING

Do you act differently around your friends than around your grandparents? How about when you're in math class or on the soccer field? Most people change the way they act based on their surroundings. Rocks are the same way!

When the conditions around a rock change, the rock changes in order to **adapt** to the new conditions, such as a higher temperature. Metamorphism is the changing of a rock's **chemical** or **physical** makeup. Metamorphic rock is the result of several kinds of metamorphism.

SET IN STONE

All metamorphic rock forms from existing rock.

Metamorphic rock is one of the three kinds of rock.
The others are sedimentary rock and igneous rock.

MAKING MOVES

Metamorphic rocks are most easily found in places where rock undergoes extreme changes, such as areas with many **earthquakes** and **volcanoes**. These places are often at the edges of the slow-moving **plates** of rock that make up Earth's surface. As they shift, one plate may force another plate deeper underground or lift it up to face rain and other weather.

Metamorphic rocks form in places with less intense condition changes as well. However, their metamorphism is harder to see and slower paced.

SET IN STONE

The word "metamorphism" comes from Greek words that mean "change of form."

Metamorphic changes occur in many places on Earth. They're most easily seen in places where two plates meet, such as the San Andreas Fault in California.

One of the most common changeable conditions that affects metamorphism is temperature. The lowest temperature that might cause metamorphic changes is about 300°F (150°C). The highest is about 2,190°F (1,200°C).

Changes in stress and pressure can also cause metamorphism. Stress is force applied to rock. It may squeeze or stretch a rock by pressing on just one or two sides of it. Pressure is uniform stress, or when the same force is used on all parts of the rock.

SET IN STONE

Sometimes stress causes rocks to change shape. This metamorphism is called strain.

Scientists can tell a lot about changes in conditions just by looking at a metamorphic rock. For example, they could guess how fast a temperature change occurred.

Metamorphic rocks usually form as a result of changes in a combination of conditions. But the changing conditions are only part of a metamorphic rock's story. Metamorphism also depends on what **minerals** are in the rock. Some minerals only melt at very high temperatures. Others break easily.

Metamorphism occurs in order to keep a rock's chemical makeup **stable** in new conditions. In some cases, the minerals have to completely change! In others, they may just shift into different forms of the same minerals.

SET IN STONE

In the right conditions, minerals grow crystals. Often, when a mineral breaks down during metamorphism, its crystals will reform in a different way. They also may not grow back at all!

Hot water and mineral mixtures flow into open spaces in rock and leave behind matter that may cause chemical changes. Yellowstone National Park has metamorphic rocks that formed this way.

REGIONAL METAMORPHISM

Regional metamorphism happens over a large area, or region, when bodies of rock, such as the plates the continents are on, move past or crash into each other. The rock is lifted up or pushed deeper into Earth. There are commonly increases in temperature and pressure as well as changes in stress and strain to cause regional metamorphism.

Metamorphic rock that forms this way can often be found in the heart of mountain ranges. Their form comes from the folding and stress on these large areas of rock.

SET IN STONE

The chemical makeup of metamorphic rock is commonly close to that of its "parent" rock. The parent rock is the existing rock that undergoes metamorphism.

Some of the metamorphic rock found in the Appalachian Mountains formed when the North American plate and African plate crashed together millions of years ago.

CONTACT METAMORPHISM

When melted rock from within Earth, or magma, flows into or near solid rock, contact metamorphism can occur. The magma's high temperature heats the cooler rock. This often happens close to Earth's surface. It's sometimes called local metamorphism because it happens in a small area.

Like all metamorphism, contact metamorphism can cause a range of changes. The rock nearest to the magma becomes very hot, and it changes to rock called hornfels. The farther away from the heat of the magma, the less a rock will change.

Hornfels is a fine-grained metamorphic rock.
What it's made up of depends on what kind of rock it started as.

15

FOLIATION

From slate to marble, there are many kinds of metamorphic rock—and they can look very different from each other! Scientists use a rock's chemical makeup to figure out what kind of metamorphic rock it is.

Another way to recognize a metamorphic rock is by its **texture**. Rocks with a foliated texture have many minerals in them that are arranged in layers and bands. Nonfoliated metamorphic rocks have one to just a few minerals in them that are hard to see individually.

SET IN STONE

Shock or impact metamorphism happens when a heavenly body, like a comet, hits Earth, or a volcano explodes very forcefully.

Gneiss has a foliated texture. Its minerals are separated in bands you can see.

WHAT KIND IS IT?

Even if you know texture and mineral makeup, metamorphic rocks are commonly hard to group. There are so many conditions that can cause metamorphism, and they can all work in combination with each other and happen in a range of ways.

Additionally, each existing rock that undergoes metamorphism acts differently because of the minerals in it. For example, two rocks may go through the same increase in temperature and pressure, but respond in their own way based on the minerals' properties.

SET IN STONE

After undergoing the same kind of metamorphism, it's possible for rocks to end up looking the same—even if they don't have the same kind of parent rock!

Slate is one kind of metamorphic rock.
It commonly forms from clay under low pressures and temperatures.

SCHIST AND GNEISS

Two common kinds of metamorphic rock—schist and gneiss—show just how hard metamorphic rock classification can be. Both of these can form from more than one kind of metamorphism and more than one kind of rock. In fact, the rocks we call schist can form from igneous, sedimentary, or metamorphic rocks!

Metamorphic rocks are some of the most amazing in the world. By studying these rocks' special bands and chemical makeup, scientists can tell us more about how Earth came to be as it is today.

schist

WHY DOES METAMORPHIC ROCK FORM?

plates or other large rock bodies meet

magma flows into or near rock

conditions around rock change, including heat, pressure, stress, or strain

magma's high temperature heats cooler rock

rock changes (physically, chemically, or both) to stay stable in new conditions

GLOSSARY

adapt: to change to suit conditions

chemical: relating to matter that can be mixed with other matter to cause changes

earthquake: a shaking of the ground caused by the movement of Earth's crust

mineral: matter in the ground that forms rocks

physical: having to do with natural science

plate: one of the large pieces of rock that make up Earth's outer layer

stable: not likely to change suddenly or greatly

texture: in geology, the size of a mineral's crystals or grains in the rock

volcano: an opening in a planet's surface through which hot, liquid rock sometimes flows

FOR MORE INFORMATION

Books

Allen, Nancy Kelly. *Slate and Other Metamorphic Rocks*. New York, NY: PowerKids Press, 2009.

Aloian, Molly. *What Are Metamorphic Rocks?* New York, NY: Crabtree Publishing, 2011.

Websites

Metamorphic Rock Gallery
geology.about.com/od/more_metrocks/ig/metamorphics/
See pictures of many kinds of metamorphic rocks and read more about how they form.

Types of Rocks
www.kidsloverocks.com/html/types_of_rocks.html
Read about all three types of rock as well as how to start a rock collection.

INDEX